Contents

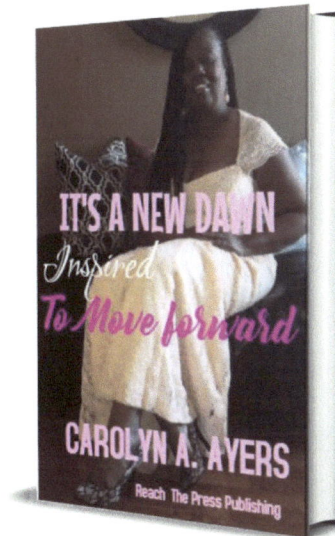

La'Shaes
WOMEN EMPOWERMENT MOVEMENT

For more information contact:cartering2women@gmail.com

| website
ladylashaes.com

Write
And
Read

With
Reach The Press
Publishing

Authors Retreat

Host

Author Jonnie Dauphine
Author Shalara Wells

Old School, 210 Railroad Ave, Loreauville, LA 70552

Date June 2nd at 1pm until 5pm

Inspiring Writers Class

Guest Speaker
Carolyn Ayers

Music
Refreshment

And much much more.......

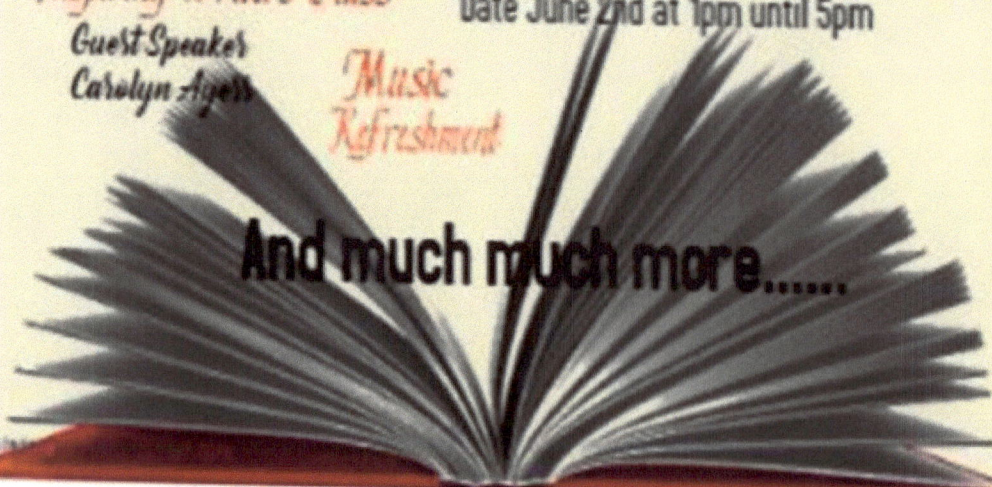

Carolyn A. Ayers

WRITING

Creative writing is any form of writing which is written with creativity in mind; Fiction writing, poetry writing, creacive non-fiction writing and more. The purpose is to express somthing, whether it be feelings, thoughts, or emotion.

Reach The Press
Publishing

REACH THE PRESS CREATED FOR WRITERS

Reach The Press was created for those who are seeking to become a publishes author. This is a way for my Non-Profit to give back to the community by providing those who are creative writers. Allowing them an opportunity to express their thoughts, life experiences, the exciting places they have traveled or just imagination or visualized stories they want to tell. Reach The Press will help them make their dream a reality.

This issue of Hidden Gems and Jewels Magazine is featuring three authors that had their book published by Reach The Press. Jonnie Dauphine, Stacey Bulluck, and Michelle Duplessis.

If you want to become an author, you have to just start writing down your creative thoughts on paper. Once you have placed them in a journal that you can refer back to then you can start putting them together and create a fantastic story for your readers. If you're looking to be the next five-star author, contact Reach The Press CEO at carolynayers@comcast.net.

Author
Jonnie Dauphine

Hidden Gems & Jewels

REACH THE PRESS PUBLISHING
PRESENTS

DANGEROUS DANA

Bad Girl Don't Mess with Me

BY: JONNIE DAUPHINE

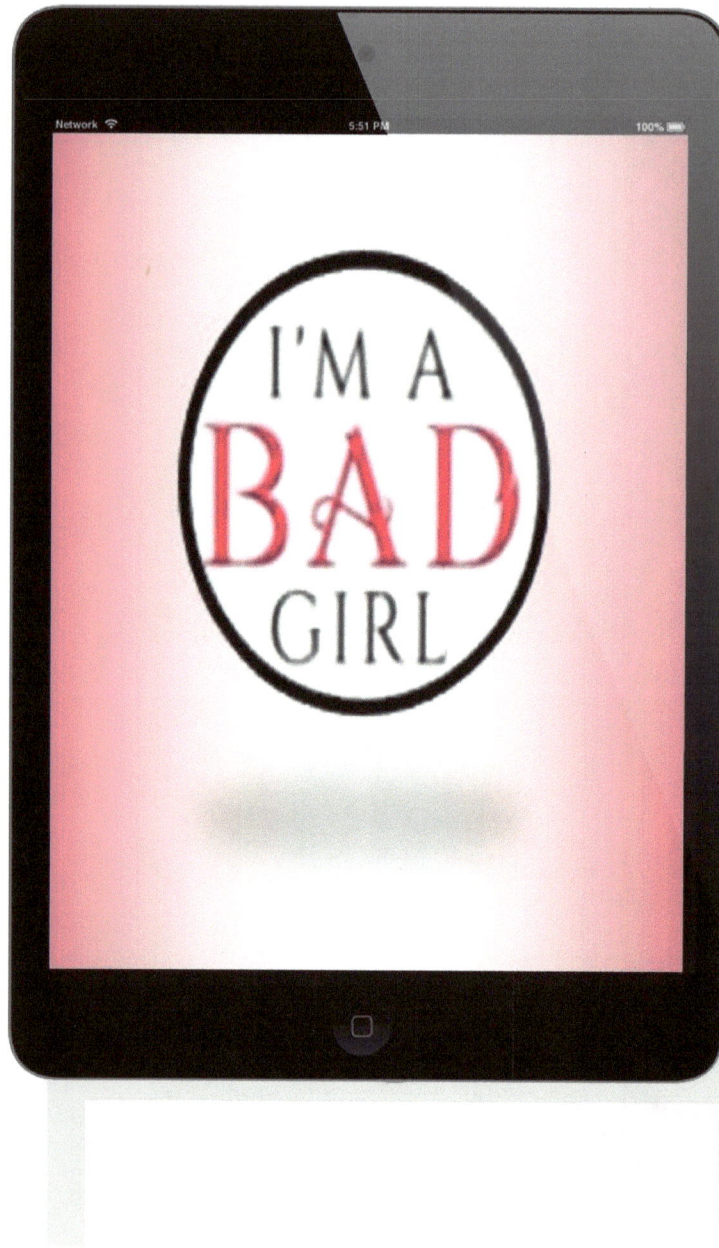

Dangerous Dana
Don't Mess with Me!

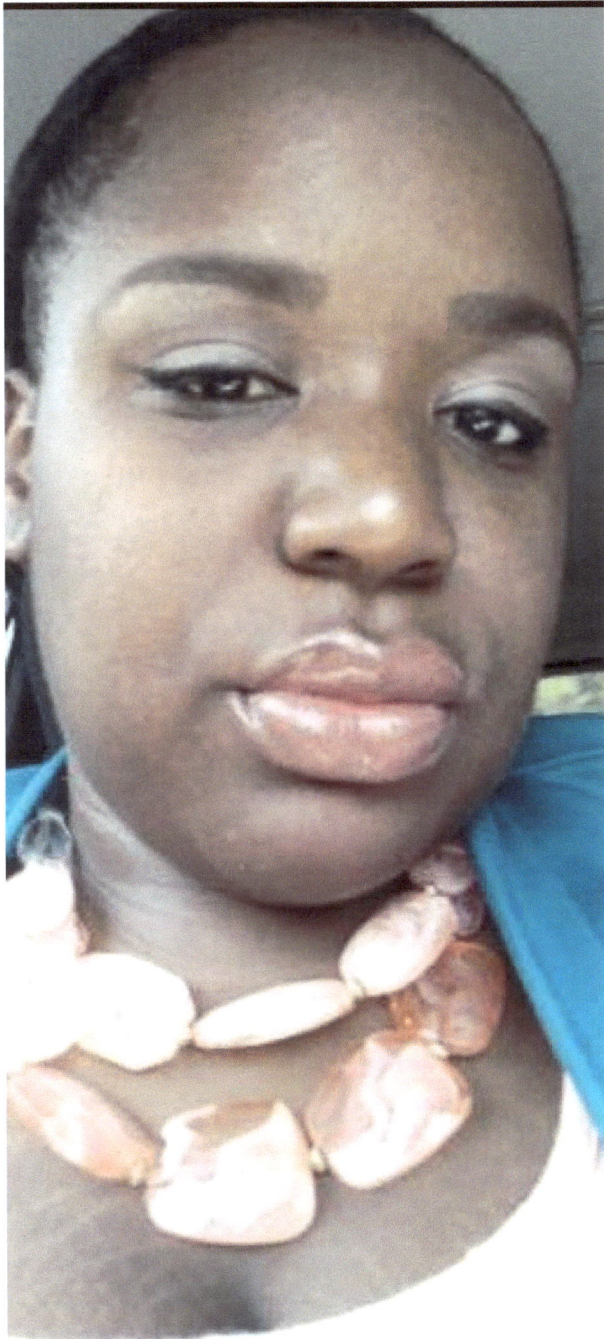

MEET THE AUTHOR

JONNIE DAUPHINE

It's like I can be who I want, say what I want, and do what I want. Writing is my freedom. It's my tool I use to fight through my tough times." Jonnie says when asked why she enjoys writing so much. Jonnie Dauphine is the definition of a southern belle, born and raised in south Louisiana. She is one of five kids, which are all boys. Growing up in the country raised around boys was not that easy, but Mrs. Dauphine prides herself on being able to keep up with a football game, shoot a shotgun, mud ride on ATVs, and still be able to get dressed up wear a full face of makeup and dress. She has been married to her adoring husband, Clifford Dauphine, for almost three years. They do not have kids yet but plan to have them soon, they have four dogs who they love to pieces. Dangerous Dana is Jonnies first published book. The book is about a young lady named Alissa, who suffered abuse as a child, developed a split personality. Alissa finds herself betrayed by her lover and best friend. Her other character Dana loved Alissa and hated to see her upset. Dana takes control of the situation, and it turns deadly. Dangerous Dana is a thrilling and captivating story that will have you wanting more. Jonnie plans on writing a sequel to Dangerous Dana that she anticipates coming out early 2020. Jonnie also is working on other writing ventures and events to help people 2 that are interested in the writing process. One of her biggest goals in life is to be the bestselling author and to help as many as she can along the way. Don't forget to get your copy of Dangerous Dana from Amazon, Wal-Mart. or Books-A-Million.

Hidden Gems & Jewels

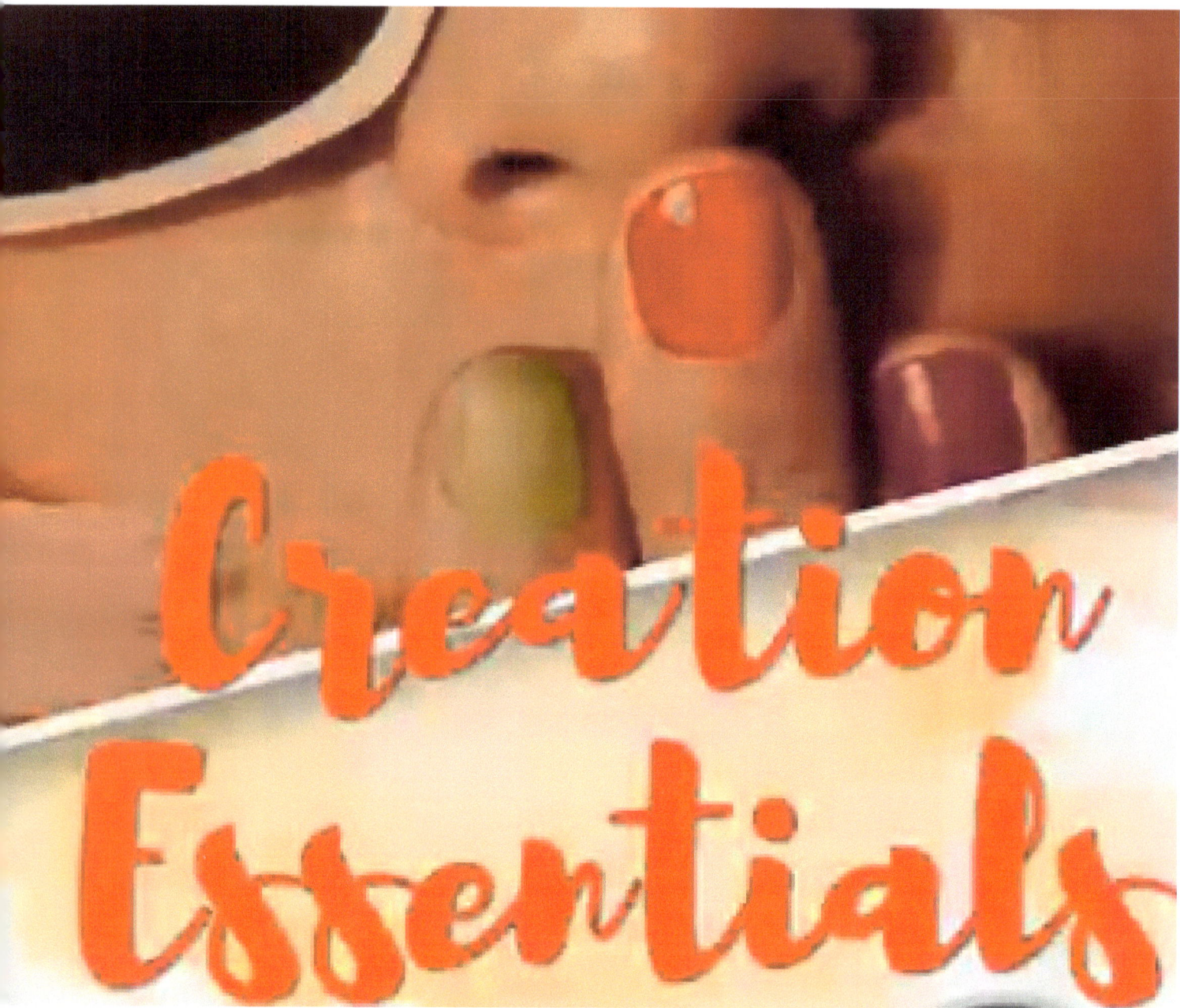

Creation Essentials

CEO
Mrs. L. Anderson

Hidden Gems & Jewels

Creation Essentials

Natural Body Products

CEO Mrs. L. Anderson

Hidden Gems & Jewels

Shawntee's

La Shaes

Lady
Butterfly

Fashion for Queens!
Shawntee's Wardrobe

Author
Michelle Duplessis

Author
Michelle Duplessis

Michelle Duplessis a native of New Orleans, Louisiana and expressed that writing her book she hopes it will be a help to the reader in making changes in their life.

God Purpose and Plan for Me
The Storm is Over Now

Ms. Duplessis stated that she is first a Woman of God a Minister, Mother, Nana, Author, Photographer, and Baker and still going.

Ms. Duplessis says life has ups and downs, most of all it is a learning and growing process. Don't give up on your dreams and always reach for the stars. Don't settle, honor and respect are critical, learning how to submit to authority and walk in obedience are so important. On your journey and being pleasing in God's eyes keep the faith and don't question when God moves people out of your life.

Quote: from Ms. Duplessis regarding her book God Purpose and Plan for Me:

An easy to follow" and "easy to read" and "promoting progress". My book is not appealing to everyone–but to the perfect reader, it's very appealing because it clearly articulates a real problem and how to overcome and enhance your life.

Ms. Duplessis book is found on Amazon.

The Storm is Over!

Bruised but not Broken

GOD HAD A PURPOSE AND PLAN FOR ME

Michelle T. Duplessis

Reach The Press Publishing

FEAR

Women of Distinction, Inc.

Don't allow fear to cloud your beautiful day.
To keep you from believing you can sore. Don't
let fear blind you when you see wrong and
keep silent when your life or your child life
depends on it...

Prophetess Carolyn Ayers

Regain Power Through Resilience

DONT LET YOUR

Brain

GO NUMB

Regret

Abuse

Rejection

Negative

Pain

Author
Stacey Bulluck

Hidden Gems & Jewels

MEET TWO TIME AUTHOR

Stacey Bulluck

Author Stacey Bulluck expressed in herbook she was going along on this journey and came to notice that she had no joy, nor did she have the ability to create happiness for herself. Stacey said that her life could have been described using the first stanza of Sade's song "Soldier of Love." The lyrics are, "I've lost the use of my heart, but I'm still alive." Her heart had been snuffed out, and she felt helpless and depleted. She was numb. Life will bring its stuff, and she want to help with the process of being prepared when the tornadic winds blow. This book will provide some tools needed for building your permanent plan to fulfill the purpose and help gain a clear understanding about what it will take to become unstuck, walk in freedom and be the prolific human being you were created to be.

Stacey Bulluck book can be found on Amazon.

Regain Power Through Resilience

DONT LET YOUR
Brain
GO NUMB

Regret

Abuse

Rejection

Negative

Pain

Harmful Words

Disappointment

Mental Pain

Belittle

Discouragement

Hate

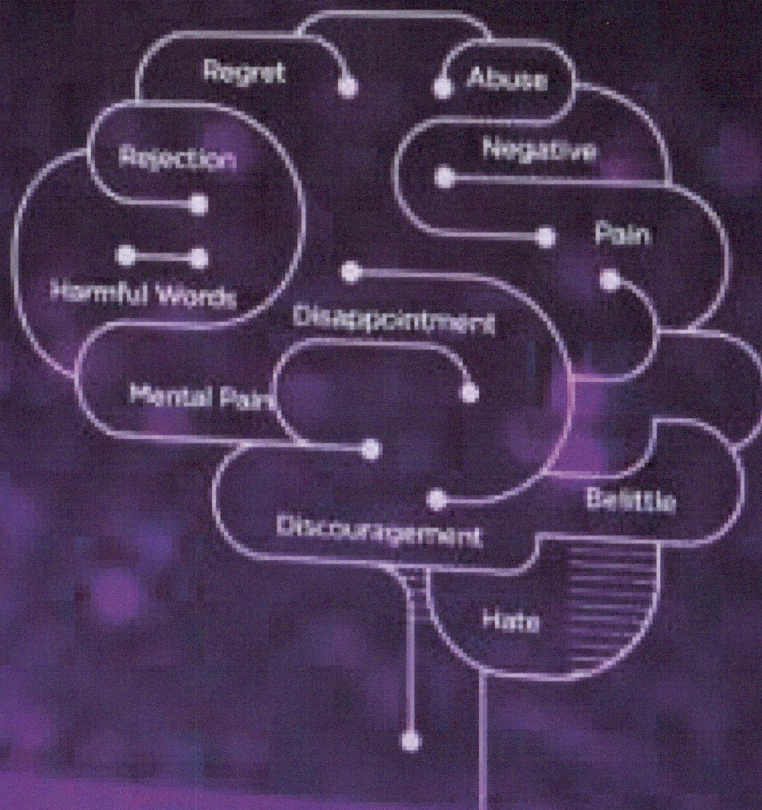

STACEY BULLUCK

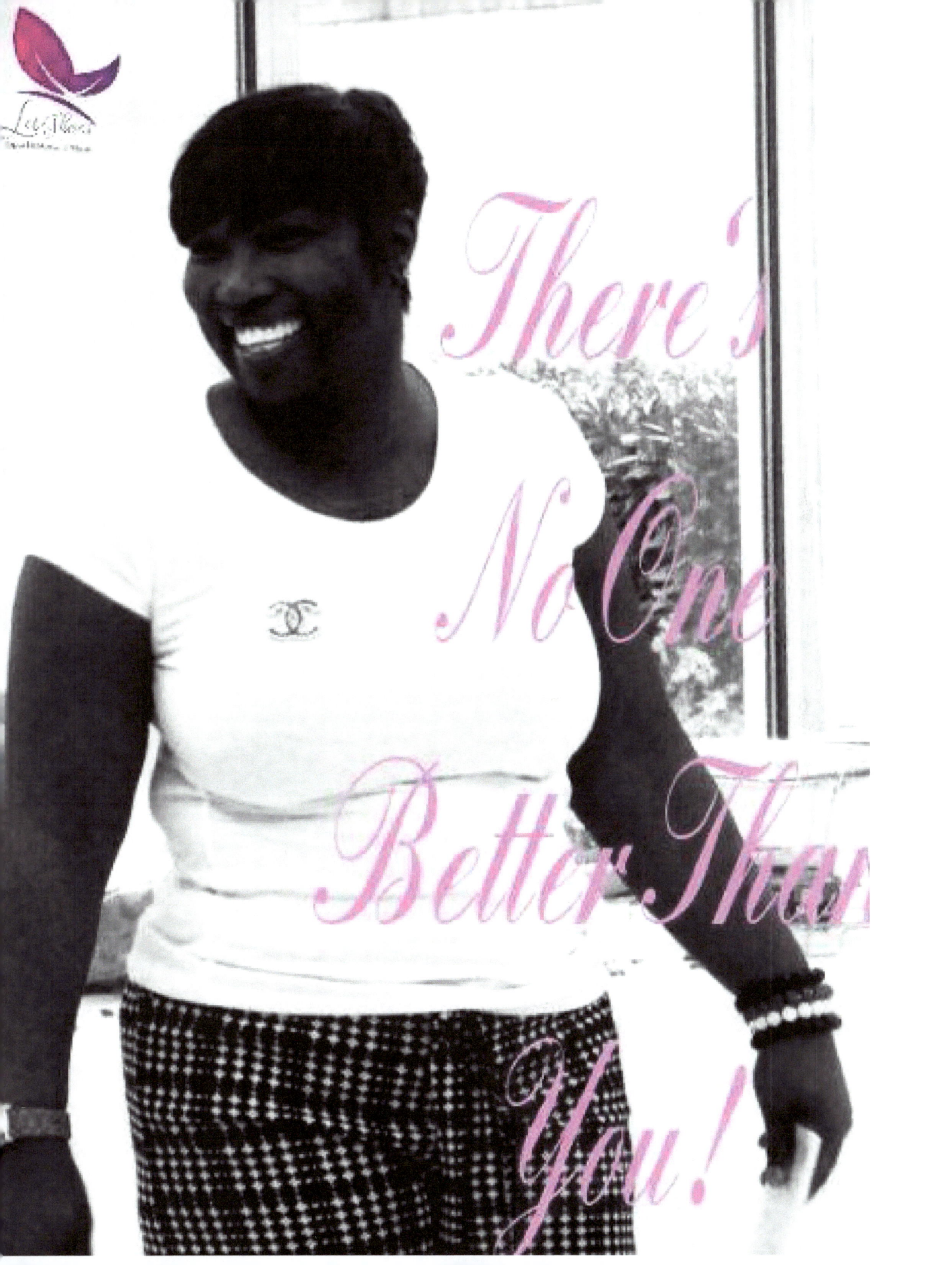

There's
No One
Better Than
You!

Inspirational Rapper Project MC

Inspirational Rapper Project MC

Poject MC is a native of Washington, DC he resides in Bowie, MD. He is a student at Bowie State University studing Broadcasting Journalism/Communication.

MC Royalty

This article is to thank him for his amazing showcase of his talent.

Insprirational Rapper/Song Writer. Peace and positivity is what he represent. Project MC was a featured guest at the 2019 La'Shaes Business Extravaganza in Houston, Texas. Where he performed at the Author Showcase event on Thursday night and the Business Couples, Night Gala on Friday night. Project MC is a outstanding performer and gave our audience an amazing show.

Wow! We was so touched by your outstanding performs. The memories will not be forgotten--and we'll think of your inspirational song everytime we think of you.

Thank you for adding to the joy and excitement of our business event with your amazing heartfelt performs. We love having you and look forward to future endeavors.

Find Project MC on Facebook

Author
Carolyn A. Ayers
Reach The Press Publishing

W O D
Women of Distinction
Women Making A Difference

Queen Valor

Five Time Author
Carolyn A. Ayers

Hidden Gems & Jewels

Carolyn A. Ayers
Five Time Author
Inspirational/ Motivational Speaker

Carolyn Ayers is a motivational speaker that impels her audience to make a change in their life, she urges them to move forward by the exertion of inspirational words promoting moral discipline.

It's A New Dawn

It's A New Dawn is heartwarming excerpts of the life of Ms. C. as she told it. The story brings you into the hurt, pain, and mistakes that Ms. Ayers made along her life journey. Ms. Ayers expounds on why she hates her dad and how it affected her life. This is a must read that will warm your heart while bringing you to tears as Ms. C express the touchstone events of her life adventure.

Ms. Ayers stated that "It's A New Dawn" will walk you through her life excursions. Giving you a glimpse of her life as a child and how those turn of events played a part in her bad decision making. Writing for Ms. Ayers is her get-a-way time from all of life challenges. She can take her mind off of the day to day grind and think about how she could touch one life by putting her emotion in print. Hoping that something from one of her books can make a difference in some ones life.

All five of Ms. Ayers books can be found and purchase on Barns Noble, Books A Million and Amazon and her magazine can be purchase on Lulu.com.

Hidden Gems & Jewels

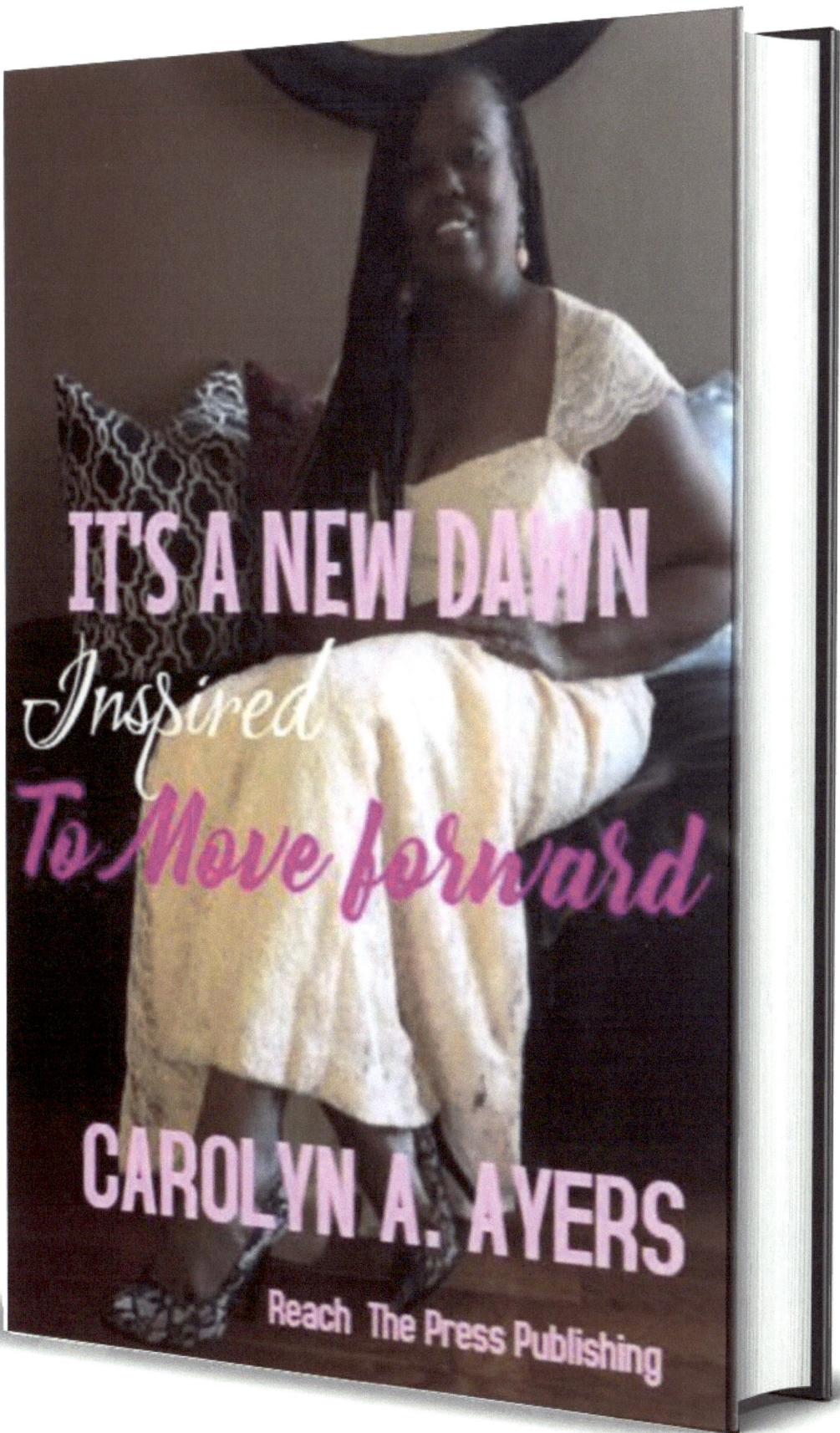

IT'S A NEW DAWN
Inspired
To Move forward

CAROLYN A. AYERS

Reach The Press Publishing

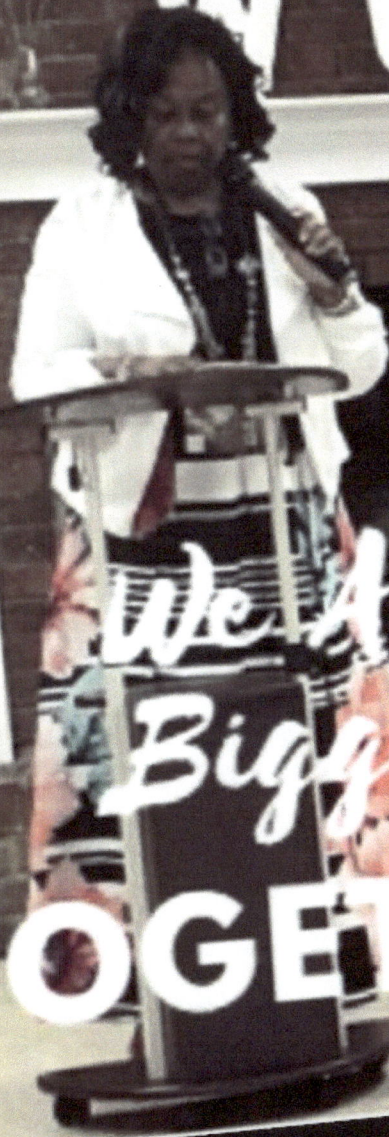

CEO

Chief Executive Officer
Carolyn A. Ayers

Own the Vision

Provide the Proper Resources

Build the Culture

Make Great Decisions

Oversee the company's Performance

WOMEN OF DISTINCTION

Women Making A Diffence